Tracy Fitzgibbons is 53 years old, a PT worker who lives in Hampshire. When not working, Tracy loves to be outdoors, gardening especially. Tracy likes spending time with her trusted friends, watching movies and practising meditation (which helped her overcome substance abuse, her fears and anxiety issues). Tracy supports many charities, believing it is her turn now to give back, for the help she herself received in getting her to where she is today. Although Tracy constantly strives to find balance and order in life, Tracy is the first to admit that she is truly the dizziest person she knows… At least, so far.

Stacie xx

I love you, Am Proud of the Amazing & Beautiful Lady you have become xx …..

Love Always

Tracy xx
Fitzgibbons xx

This book is dedicated to

My angel brother, JOHN PAUL BERRY, who walks beside me still inspiring and guiding me on my journey.

This book is dedicated to the lost souls everywhere.

Tracy Fitzgibbons

THE SOUL SCENE

AUSTIN MACAULEY PUBLISHERS™
LONDON • CAMBRIDGE • NEW YORK • SHARJAH

Copyright © Tracy Fitzgibbons 2023

The right of Tracy Fitzgibbons to be identified as author of this work has been asserted by the author in accordance with sections 77 and 78 of the Copyright, Designs and Patents Act 1988.

All rights reserved. No part of this publication may be reproduced, stored in a retrieval system, or transmitted in any form or by any means, electronic, mechanical, photocopying, recording, or otherwise, without the prior permission of the publishers.

Any person who commits any unauthorised act in relation to this publication may be liable to criminal prosecution and civil claims for damages.

A CIP catalogue record for this title is available from the British Library.

ISBN 9781035801107 (Paperback)
ISBN 9781035801114 (Hardback)
ISBN 9781035801121 (ePub e-book)

www.austinmacauley.com

First Published 2023
Austin Macauley Publishers Ltd®
1 Canada Square
Canary Wharf
London
E14 5AA

To JACKY my mystical, magical, tarot-reading friend

Without your insight and your gifts, I would still be wandering lost…And this book would never be. You truly are a remarkable 'witch-woman'
Thank you so much, for everything.

To PETER BERRY Thank you for my computer, so I could write (…And for teaching me how to use the damned thing)!

To KEVIN HEGGARTY Thank you for being the best friend I could ever have wished for. For all your love and constant support, I am eternally grateful.

(… And for believing in me when no one else did, not even myself)
Words could not express how much I love you.
You are my rock and I would be lost without you.

To ALL THE PEOPLE I HAVE MET ON MY JOURNEY…
THANK YOU FOR THE LESSONS.

THE SOUL SCENE (or *SOUL SEEN*, working title) is a collection of experiences that we, as individuals, all experience, love, loss, loneliness, losing our way, losing our mind, our faith and even our dreams as we navigate ourselves through life. It illustrates the struggles that we all feel, that we all have in our daily lives. Those struggles where we feel alone or the need to keep things private in fear of judgement. It is a reminder that WE have power inside, that we are not alone and helpless. That we are not isolated or weird or stuck… We are souls living the human experience. We can change ourselves, our lives, others' lives, and together we could change the world to make a better, less destructive society… But that journey begins inside. By slowing down long enough, to ask: who am I, am I happy, do I create positivity or negativity around me, for others, and why do I keep making the same mistakes and never find the happiness I seek.

Soul Scene is what I see when I look around me, what I have experienced and what I have learnt… so far. Hello, I am Tracy. I am 53 years young. I only started to live two years ago when, through a few encounters, my perception changed. I had grown up in a narcissistic family (no judgement now) who never managed to break the genetic traits passed on down from generation to generation. Most with drug or alcohol issues, etc., etc. I smoked pot to run from the pain, the mistakes and lack of understanding. Two years ago, I stopped all the running. Dealt with the shadows, got clean (not even cigarettes). Today, my life is so much better. I write (therapy) and work. I enjoy life. I am hoping that sharing my life experiences may just resonate with another lost traveller and maybe, just maybe, help their light to shine, that little bit brighter. For without the love and advice I was given, who knows where I would be today. Life guides us, sends us lessons as we live in the *Soul Scene*. Once we transcend our ego, our pain, our fears and our false perceptions, life does get better.

I have been writing about 13 to 14 months now. The only things published are *LOCKDOWN Poem* in Portsmouth evening news on July 1st 2021 and *SPRING, SUMMER, AUTUMN, WINTER poems,* published in GOSPORT BOROUGH COUNCIL'S Tennant Magazine.

Thank you all for taking the time to read my poems.

Tracy Fitzgibbons.

The Soul Scene

Welcome to your journey
To birth, on Earth's soul scene.
You've chose, to learn, experience
To know, what living means.

Each soul has their mission
To aspire to, when born.
Each will face set challenges
Whilst dressed, in human form.

You will come to find
Earth is a complicated place.
Designed to blind you from your truth
Test your strength of faith.

All will live, surrounded
By countless challenged souls.
Here, in this Karmic playground
As they try to reach their goals.

Nobody works together
There's disconnect in the collective.
With harmony of balance tipped
Negatively, all's affected.

As pressure to survive distracts
You'll forget your objectives.
Lose touch with your power
Feel emotionally dejected.

Lessons will present to guide you
Through this human maze.
Success will be dependent
On the choices that are made.

As you adopt your mortal form
Your memory's erased.
But, deep inside, you'll feel it
Something's missing, been misplaced.

So, welcome to your journey
Find your path, face life's extremes
By the time you have endured it all,
You'll know what living means.

Love

Can you show me love?
Can you place it in your hand?
Have you proof of its power
Why its potency commands?

Everybody's searching
In hope to capture love.
This force, indeterminate
Source, we are in need of.

Love cannot be claimed
It is a gift we are Entrust!
When you recognise this truth
Then love, it chooses us.

If you wish to find love
First, you have to be Loving.
If you do not, give of yourself
Then what's returned is nothing!

Love has many facets
Compassion, faith and trust.
It nurtures and reveals our heart
Creates a life that's just.

Love can forge such strength
Before its touch – you never had.
Gives courage and shows temperance
Transforms the heart that's flagged.

Love is peace, enduring
Love teaches, elevates.
Let love be your cause
To live, let your heart generate.

Love is everywhere you'll find
Change perception, you will see.
What you seek, before – was yours
It's inside you and me.

Love is unconditional
A divine transforming force.
If you use its power wisely,
Then, your heart will be endorsed.

Karma

Every thought and deed you craft, one day, returns to you
The life you're living here and now, causal effect accrued.
If history repeats itself, Karma's serving lessons due
Only when you own your truth, can there be a
Breakthrough!

Life just doesn't happen, get involved, accept your role
To co-create in your life, live each moment in life's flow.
Recognise your heart's desire, shine truth upon your soul
To honour your authentic self, foremost should be you goal.

Resist dark, hostile energies that restrain, encumber you
Live free of shame, past regret, make way for something
New.
Disconnect yourself, from what no longer will serve you
Make positive vibration the intention that you use.

Detach from limiting beliefs, empower new reactions
Cause yourself to generate life-enhancing interactions.
Give to that, which you believe, with conscientious action
Create a better road to walk, live life with satisfaction.

You may think your efforts won't mean that much at all
But all energy's connected, however big or small.
You can make a difference in the grand scheme of it all
What you choose, cause consequence – the rising and the Fall.

We all have our unique gifts, inside we've got the lot
With challenges of earthly form, sometimes our faith is Knocked.
Trust universal force, its frequency will help unblock
Aligned to higher power, know that we cannot be stopped.

Be gracious and be humble in everything you do
The more effort you invest, the more comes back to you.
Everybody has their own path; it's something they must Choose
Your duty is to redefine the best version of you.

Have patience, be consistent; reaching destiny takes time. Our journey keeps on changing; it could take us 'all-our-Lives'. Believe in yourself always, question that, which would deny.
For, You'll ever walk in circles, if you don't dare To try.

Tears

Tears that fall
Reveal my heart
Within its silent flow.

Shrouded wounds
Release and cleanse
In drops of indigo.

As waterfalls
Aid greetings to
My loving heart, unknown.

I will not try
To stem the tide
For, as I weep, I grow.

Light Shine

Let your light shine brightly
Let your soul illuminate.
Let the power of its source
Give strength to radiate.

Let your light's expression
Bear kindness in your eyes.
Let the light within your heart
Touch those as you pass by.

Let your light's inspiration
Be example for us all.
Let your light shine, uplift
Ignite its spark in all.

Let your light be of service
To raise, help those who fall.
Let your light be rays of hope
That aids to every call.

Let your light be blinding
May it serve and protect you!
Let it keep you from the dark
Help you live your life true.

Let your light foster courage
When you walk the road alone.
Let your light guide your journey
Then, be your compass home.

Little One

Hello there, little one
Hey… I remember you!
I'm sorry it has been so long
The years have flown; it's true.

Do you recognise me
Though I do not look the same?
How could I have forgotten?
You've waited, I'm to blame.

Remember, many years ago
When hopes and dreams were young?
We thought we were invincible
We chased the summer sun.

Laughter was our pastime
Imagination prompted fun.
We thought we could do anything
…Could become anyone.

Not sure how it happened
How you got left behind.
Forgive me, for neglecting
Your heart and soul… Not kind!

In eagerness to come of age
Somehow, I abandoned you.
In thinking I knew better
…Deafened to your point of view.

Recognised – you were hurt
Left lonely, feeling spurned.
How patiently you've waited
For my fated, return.

I'll try to fix our discord
Through hard lessons I have learnt.
I promise, never, will I leave again
…When I finally return.

I'll pray you will forgive me
Help me heal the pain.
It's only us that suffer
As we, remain estranged.

Little one, still waiting
…In a picture, in a frame.
Still searching, for a way back
To reconnect again.

Lockdown

Lockdown? The fears abound, as people started falling
Down.
COVID spread throughout the land, indiscriminate of
Races.
Quickly it went GLOBAL! There were no more safe
Places!

A PLANETARY PANDEMIC... PANIC! A reported
Hundred thousand cases
The figure rises every day... Incredulous, frightened-
looking faces.
Everyone was buying face masks, everyone now
Sanitised
Except for some, who just believed, "It's all a pack of
Lies!"

In care homes and establishments, the cared for were cut
Down.
Outside, their families cried for them
They weren't allowed too near.
They were denied, one last goodbye, to the loved ones
they held dear.

The masses, they were sent home, furloughed paid 80%.
Kids became home-schooled, parents' patience came and
Went.

All non-essential businesses were told to shut their
doors.
Economies forced to liquidate, some gone for evermore.
The airports too affected, planes sat idle on the floor.
…When would things return to normal and service be
restored?
No one had the answers, so no one knew for sure!

For many, they watched Netflix, ordered take-out on the
Phone.
For some, it was harder, felt imprisoned in their home.
The stresses of confinement brought within this situation
reported highs of fights, abuse, depression, desperation.
As thousands died every week, our mental health was
failing.

We queued at supermarkets in controlled two-meter
zones
whilst we were on 'the hunt' for the 'elusive toilet rolls'.
The streets and roads were vacant, just flying
Ambulances wailing…
Inside another fearful patient, whose lungs had started
Ailing.

The N.H.S. was under pressure, getting close to breaking
point.

The sick, they kept arriving; hospitals were inundated.
Healthcare staff – they rallied, though they felt enervated.
They 'suited-up' worked nonstop; they watched their Colleagues fall.
Paramedics and researchers, doctors, nurses, midwives, all…
We truly owe you our lives
GOD BLESS and THANKYOU, ALL!

Mother Nature has reminded us; she really is the boss.
For those that didn't make it through, so sorry for your loss.

Perfect Lives

There are so many out there, oh, you perfect wives!
With perfect homes and families, your car's the perfect
Ride.
Yes, it seems you've made it good, You've got the
Perfect life!
How fulfilled you must be… you lucky, lucky wife.

To the unknown onlooker, to the neighbours, yes, it
seems
You realised your vision, you are living your own
dream.
No doubt you worked so hard throughout, in life, to get
this far
You gave the very best of you, you grafted, moulded,
saved.
You should be proud; the credit's yours… you really
Have it made.

For some of you (the lucky few) still live in wedded bliss
With sex 'still on the table' not just something that you
Miss.

For most of you (you know who), there's an underlying
Tone
As your key turns, in your front door, you're feeling
Quite alone.
In your castle, no more laughter (never mind orgasmic
Moans)
You console yourself with wine, chat with your friends
On the phone.

If your man is just a shadow, of the promise he once
was. If it seems, his only interests are computer, golf and
pub.
If his snoring is the only thing, these days, that rocks
Your bed.
Perhaps, it's time you traded in, got yourself loved
instead.
… Or maybe take some time away to clarify your head.

Aren't you tired of pretending that everything's alright?
The atmosphere, the silence, the stresses and the fights.
The tears you cry alone are symptoms of the situation
Release yourself from the pain. Ease your slow stagnation.

Of course money's nice, but it won't keep you warm at
Night
Yes, change is always scary, but, things will work out
Right.
It doesn't mean you've failed to turn from all this
Aggravation
Not if you know there is no chance of reconciliation.

You are stronger. You are braver than in your
Imaginations
Take charge… Be gladiatorial! You can shape your
Destination.
Expel the fear that binds you to this indifferent station
What will you choose? It's up to you, inaction or salvation.

Don't try to live the perfect life, that's all just an illusion.
The only truth worth living for is love's pure, sweet
infusion.
There are so many out there, whose hearts remain unfed.
… So, choose your poison wisely
… Well, you know… enough said!

Dark Days

In these dark days,
It's so hard to love.
We all struggle on
These times, they are tough!

We get caught in the chaos
Our fight to survive.
Our mental poise attenuates
Our hearts desensitise.

We relinquish our faith
Our hopes, our dreams.
The doubts residing inside
Steal in which we believe.

Disregard the demon
That whispers in your ear

"You are not good enough!"
"You do not belong!"
"You do not deserve!"
"Give up… You're not strong!"

LOVE YOURSELF. YOU'RE BEAUTIFUL!
BE COURAGEOUS. BE FORGIVING!
Bear NO shame. We are all the SAME
We ALL have our misgivings!

REACH OUT, SPEAK! RELEASE the PAIN!
…Of self-judgement, reminiscing.
FREE YOURSELF. STAKE YOUR CLAIM!
CHOOSE TO STRIVE. START LIVING!

Wake Up

People, it is time to think
Look at the world we're making.
Our souls are heavy, languishing
… Instead of elevating.

Everyone is hooked in
Cultured by the internet.
Feeding off the cyber stream
As dreams remain unmet.

We are living our existence
As per electric protocol.
With detriment, it's aiding
The individual's downfall.

Unplug yourself, free up your brain
For independent thinking.
Society should not slave to this pixel screen
We're binging.

Instead of clicking 'follow'
Or 'liking' something else…
Take the lead in your own life
Choose something for yourself.

Wake up and remember
Who you truly are inside.
You don't need social media
To judge, to lead, to hide.

Step away from your computer
Put down your mobile phone.
The world you're sitting staring at
Starts one step from your home.

Outside, waits your own future
Go see, experience it all.
The first step to find happiness
Is one word… UNINSTALL!

Change

Mahatma Gandhi once said, "Be the change you wish to See."
Imagine just how beautiful our world could truly be.
If instead of living blind, self-obsessed and miserly
We opened up our eyes, our hearts, lived his philosophy.

We wouldn't measure success as possessions, status, cash
Selfishly concerned in gaining more and looking flash.
We wouldn't be content to pass the homeless in the street
Those deficient of a safe place or food enough to eat.

Children wouldn't grow to feel neglected and unloved
Doomed to repeat the cycle of abuse, of drink and drugs.
The wayward of the urban jungle, lost kids that carry knives
Might have had an improved future, with some mentoring in Life.

Open-mindedly, we'd disregard colour, creed or race
We would see that everyone was born from one same place.
Instead of warring with each other, divided in our factions
We would unite, champion equal rights, cause positive reactions.

Politicians would deliver, as manifestos would imply
People wouldn't feel forgotten, abandoned, patronised.
The young could feel assured in a future satisfied
Instead of battling depression, rising young male suicide.

Governments would regulate with virtuous intent
We wouldn't need to question, where were our taxes spent?
The pressures of survival would not be greatly amplified
the Gap between the have, have-nots, wouldn't seem so wide.

Industry would be accountable; hugely-fined for dumping
Waste. Pollutants wouldn't be destroying our soil, our seas,
Airspace.
If policies were reinforced with effective legislation
Sea levels wouldn't flood, causing tragic forced migration.

Infrastructures would be funded without a subjective
Mind-set
Class-dependant education would be outlawed not inbred.
Quick, lifesaving healthcare is something we'd all get.
nurses Wouldn't have to work like dogs, then cry at their
pay Checks.

We would not be trapped in our oppressive, societal cage
Used like mice, to grease the wheels, for rich men's power
Games.
Shareholders of conglomerates would redistribute its profits
Instead of stuffing even more into their bulging pockets.

No doubt, it's evidential so much needs to be addressed
We could ease all this tail-spinning, finally, see real Progress.
If everyone would take a stand, and protest-ceaselessly!
Just Remember Mr Gandhi's words…
"Choose to do it – Peacefully"

Fear

Fear is… False evidence—appearing real
It's a trick of the mind, a veil to conceal.
It's a battle within, of SOUL versus BRAIN
A lesson to be learnt, whilst here on this third plane…

One is energy-animate, our spirits boundless, immortal Force.
Our essence, our true self, our consciousness, intuition
With a capacity to transcend… if only we would listen!

The other is the operator of the soul's organic machine.
Where we find our mind and ego, and they're not working as a team
In fact, it is quite clear… one part—it's just schemes!

Our logical minds, false ego says… "You were born into your station.
This is the way that things are done
Give up your dreams. Accept your limitations…
I AM the controller of this body, this formation!"

Your inner soul knows better! Says… "No! I know what I am."
Though I am cased in skin and bone…
I am a force, am energy, I can transcend of man.
The eyes' perceived reality imprisons; it's a scam
(Just as Rene Descartes wrote)… *"I think, therefore I am!"*

Oh, the mystery, duality, of the human…being
This false-envisioned life that your ego has you seeing.
It's filled with want and daily grind-labelled failure and Success
Judgements from your false ego, keeps attention, keeps you Stressed
Insecurities and doubts? It's your ego unaddressed!

Break this cycle of control, designed to keep you active
So you don't tire, abandon will – then you won't live Reactive.
True happiness cannot be found, with momentary Satisfaction
The key to living your own dreams – first, silence the Distractions.

To separate from ego, you must have mindfulness
To reconnect with your true self, reach higher Consciousness.
You could practice yoga, or transcendental meditation
Enlightenment will guide you there and free you from Stagnation.

Live life in accordance, with the seven laws of attraction
No choice is without impact though, and that includes Inaction!
Your destiny is waiting! Inside, you hear it's calling
So, now it's time to decide to rise, or keep on stalling?

Sombre Night

Tonight, as darkness steals you
Fight against the sombre night.
Stay yourself, from this thief
That would possess your light.

The midnight blues that tempt
Give shady promise of relief.
Distorting shadows cast on you
Bewitch, with cursed beliefs.

Do not resign in wearied fight
Reject your welcome to despair.
Delve the depths of your resolve
Find mental strength to bear.

Let faith lead you to glory
Birth hope in each new day.
Hold on, for morning's sunlight
Will shine on you again.

Breathe

When you dread the day ahead
When it's tough inside your skin.
When your nights are darker than
The weather storm within.

When you feel lost, or, in too deep
Or, there is no way out.
Don't lose your cool, get overwrought
No need to scream or shout.

JUST BREATHE. Let it out, then in again.
JUST BREATHE. Take a moment to regain.
JUST BREATHE. Compose yourself; practise restrain.
JUST BREATHE. Detach yourself from the pain.
JUST BREATHE. It's just a temporary drain.

You will encounter problems
As you travel your life journey.
Sometimes, you will feel enraged
Helpless or unworthy.

It's so easy to get caught up
In emotional situations.
Intellect goes 'out the window'
As we react to our frustrations.

The key to thinking clearly
To find balance, pass each test.
Take just a few moments
Take control of your breath.

JUST BREATHE. You won't feel panicked or unnerved.
JUST BREATHE. 'Irrational' won't make things worse.
JUST BREATHE. True feelings can then be heard.
JUST BREATHE. You'll find what will suit you best.
JUST BREATHE. You will prevail with no regrets.

Your Life to Live

This is your life, for you to live
None should tell you what to do.
Though many will try to advise
It's really up to you.

Some people will be wanting for you
What they think is best.
Others will hide their true intent
Serve their own interests.

Not everyone who's friendly
You may find, is honest, nice.
Their smile could be just a disguise
Their unarming device.

Don't be cajoled or pressured
Slow down. Take time to think.
Above all else, trust in yourself
Listen to your instincts.

You are not responsible
To serve anyone else.
Firstly, your moral duty
Is to take care of yourself.

Honour your own feelings
They'll guide you from your heart.
Don't let yourself be silenced
Be strong. Be heard. Be smart.

It's really up to others
How they respond to you.
Don't let emotions blackmail
In their bid to control you.

No one can harm or disrespect
If you refuse to let them do it!
Once you learn to speak your truth
You'll see; there's nothing to it!

This is your life, for you to live
None should tell you what to do.
Those that truly love and care
Will support in what you choose.

Little Child

Oh, little child, of innocence
You failed to understand.
No warmth was found, no loving smile
No safe, nurturing hand.

Oh, little child, in loneliness
Days passed by, all alone.
The gift of time, so seldom shared
No, she was rarely home.

Oh, little child, of hopefulness
Loyal to your heart's crusade.
Time and again, you'd seek for change
But your advance was stayed.

Oh, little child, in hurtfulness
How cruelty leaves its stain.
The bitterness of angry words
Tormented you with pain.

Oh, little child, of hungriness
Your character was made.
The shadow of its yearning
Walks beside you, all your days.

Oh, little child, in wisdom
You have battled hard to grow.
You work for peace, for balance
So love may know your soul.

Oh, little child, of compassion
Be forgiving, if you would,
For, we all live within life's flow
She did just what she could.

Oh, little child, in understanding
All the darkness will be done.
You will be free, to truly see
The promise of each rising sun.

Dark Places

You're so busy getting drunk, just to live, you must be
Stoned
Your defence is… "GET STUFFED! I'M FROM A
BROKEN HOME!"
No, I am not judging. I get it. Yes, I do
(Though, memories are somewhat vague.) I used to be like
you…

I too once toked all through the night, my joints were Extra –
Grande
Dropped LSD, popped ecstasy, like a greedy kid eats candy.
I raved all night, tripped zombie-like, to house, to bass and
Drum
At the time, I thought… *I'm fine! I'm young, just having fun.*
I behaved like a rebel. I was wild child. No.1 … Yes,
I must have smoked a forest, in my day, to keep me numb!

I had to keep my demons down, the pain inside too much.
I just could not handle it, lived in the demons' clutch.
I, too, was young when broken. Was unloved, battered,
Abused
I mean, what the bloody hell was I supposed to do?!

I did not know how to change. I'd lived that way so long
Truth be told, I wasn't sure that anything was wrong! Or…
Was it just because I thought, *I'm weak, I'm not that
Strong?!*

Then one day, I heard them… Five words that changed my
Life…
(Simple yet effective) … "WHAT ARE YOU RUNNING
FROM?"

I had a 'light-bulb moment' and from that moment on… I
Knew that I could turn things round, didn't have to be
Affected. I didn't have to live my life SCREWED UP and
DISCONNECTED!

The very thing I ran from is exactly what I need
But first, I had to learn to trust, to fix where my heart
Bleeds…

You can't outrun your demon; you can't satisfy his greed.
He hides in those dark places, where there's weakness in
Your head. He powerfully taunts you, always waiting to be
Fed!
Just face your demon 'head-on' shine a light on your dark
Places
You may as well just save yourself. Put his demon ass in
Stasis!

LOVE YOURSELF. LIVE FOR YOURSELF, but, LOVE
FIRST STARTS WITH YOU! IF YOU DON'T RESPECT
YOURSELF, then, NO ONE ELSE WILL, TOO!

The world's NOT out to get you. You've carried this TOO LONG!
DON'T take the world so personally. S**T HAPPENS, just MOVE ON!
Your new life's waiting for you… TIME TO FIND WHERE You BELONG.

Mirror

As you look into the mirror, what reflection do you see?
Do you embrace your beauty? For God made you perfectly!
Are you filled with self-judgement, with image negativity?
Pursuing in false standards of cosmetics' beauty queens?

The purveyors of image so want you to believe
All their perfect products are something that you need
Shaping your perceptions, playing off low self-esteem
"If you buy our merchandise, then you can live the dream."

It's a fabricated promise. It is illusory advertising
Where everyone is happy, flawless… impossible—they're
Lying!
If you wish to find contentment, first, you must stop the rot
Acknowledge it's all make-believe, manufactured,
Photo-shopped.

Don't buy into the latest trends, the must-have latest fads
Happiness in yourself does not come with a price tag.
It is a temporary boost, a 'paid-for momentary glad'
But soon, that feeling's gone again, leaving you still sad.

Every single person struggles with self-confidence
To think you can just buy it, really makes no sense.
Of course, it's only natural to wish to look your best
You're not in competition though, no need to be obsessed.

Beauty isn't something that is painted on your skin
It is your unique light that shines from deep within.
Be kinder to yourself – free all your insecurities
Confidence will grow with you, nurtured by maturity.

It doesn't really matter, what others think or say
Love yourself, for yourself, for who you are today.
When you look into the mirror, renew your point of view
Remind yourself you're beautiful. There's no one else like
You.

The Blue

Meandering along
Floating on the blue
Cool and calm within my skin
Still waters carry through.

Peacefully suspended
I embrace the view
I am my own captain
On a solo pleasure cruise.

Suddenly, it's colder
I gaze above my head
Darkest, unexpected clouds
Descending – filled with dread.

A windstorm now encircles
I'm powerless to free
Hijacked by its violent wave
I'm thrust, lost out at sea.

I'm spinning fast, helpless
A whirlpool has me trapped
Lost all sense of direction
And my courage fails to act.

This deluge now consumes me
My submission weighs me down
Fear is released, surrendered
Calm replaces, silence found.

Above my head, it glisten's
A golden shining light
To guide me, out of darkness
And will me on to fight.

This beam of hope is warming
Reminds me, I am seen and loved.
It strengthens my resolve to rise
…That I, am worthy of.

Angels

Do you believe in angels?
That hope, eternal springs
In unicorns and rainbows
All those magical things?

They're supposed to keep you safe, you know!
And, if your faith is strong…
RELAX, CAST ASIDE YOUR FEARS
For, NOTHING CAN GO WRONG!

But, somewhere, down this road I've walked
Faith and hope betrayed me.
All that I believed in, had, somehow
Now unmade me!

Who stole my smile? Why kick me down?
I practised what was preached!
Who took my stars away from me
Then placed them out of reach?

Why tear my heart out of its skin
And throw it in the gutter?
(And whilst I'm on the subject)
Why must so many suffer?!

My light had almost faded now
My heart just barely beating…
To my surprise, out of the blue
I had the strangest meeting!

An Angel stood before me
I swear! She just appeared!
She wiped the tears from my eyes
Helped my vision clear.

She made me feel I mattered
Helped me 'back on track'.
By God, she even found my smile
And gave the damned thing back!

She helped me find the beauty
And the wonder of all things!
Isn't it amazing?
What a little kindness brings!

So, if I'm ever asked…
Do I believe in magic things?
My answer will be SURE!
… But not all angels
WEAR THEIR WINGS!

Friend

The power of a friend is remarkable indeed
If you have a good one, it's all the love you need.
A friend will show you love in so many different ways
Sometimes it's buying flowers, or it's chats with coffee
Days.

Sometimes, it's in their kindness, their forgiving little ways
Perhaps, it's just the way they make you smile
When skies are rainy-grey.

A friend will help to raise you, when you're crying, on your
Knees.
Will remind you of the beauty, of the person that They see.
A true friend will not judge you, for weakness, or
Imperfection.
If you should ever make mistakes, you need not fear
Rejection.
A friend will never shout, but, gently brings it to attention
Then gives you room to work it out with quiet introspection.

When darkest truths come flooding out, drowning out
Your soul
You can lose sight of who you are or which way you should
Go.
Your friend becomes your moral compass – a bright and
Guiding star
Reminds you to keep going, even if it seems too far.

If you lack strength or courage to swim the tidal waves of
Life
If you feel you've had enough, really can't go on… No
More…
A true friend reaches out for you, pulls you to safer shores.

A good friend, they just get you, can read you like a book.
They know just what you're thinking without the need to
Look.
The best of friends fill your heart with sunshine, love and
Laughter
Always treats you with respect, though they know… you are
Really a disaster.

They are your guardians of secrets, keepers of your trust
If you have behaved foolishly, they never bring it up.
Your friend remains a constant of tolerance and patience
Regardless – what you do or don't – give the best of
Salutations.

A friend comes armed with good advice, with wine and
Caring hugs.
Challenge you, encourage you, to reach for stars above.

They help to make good memories, co-creators of your story
All these things, they do for you
…Without the need for glory.

A true friend goes the distance, accepts you as you are
Make their mark upon your heart, with unconditional love.
They will never steal your sunshine or place you in their shadow.
Your friend gives hope, helps you believe…
In the power of tomorrow.

I Wonder

What's it like in heaven?
Do you like it? Now you're there
Did you walk through that tunnelled light?
Or ascend up Jacob's stairs?

Who came to collect you
When your time came to go home?
I hope that you have peace there
That you are not alone.

Did you have to check in
With St Peter at the gates?
Was there a queue… all waiting
To speak with God's own advocate?

What's it like? Now you've transcended
Now that your soul is free
To soar… throughout the universe
With your angel energy.

Is it really you that's talking
When you visit me, in dreams?
How time and space between us
Disappears, or least, it seems.

Have you answers to the questions
Earthly scholars cannot find
I guess those things we all find out
Each one in our own time.

Will you come to guide me
When I have seen my last sun set?
As I exhale my last breath,
I'll seek you, don't forget!

The bond of love cannot be broken
It is stronger than all things
So, until when we meet again,
To memories I shall cling.

I Walked Beside

I made you a promise that I would never leave
The sands of time would not be stayed
And now, how your heart grieves.

Though you cannot see me, know this; I can see you
I am witness to your life. I know of All you do.
Our bond is never-ending, but doubt, it captures you.

I sit right beside you, as you sit in my armchair
Hear every word you speak to me when wishing I was there.
I see every teardrop that falls when you're alone.
I see that sadness shrouds you, how much you have grown.

Try to keep your faith strong, be brave and carry on
The energy of all I am has changed, but I'm not gone.
When your sadness eases, which might take some time, I'll
send you divine signals, that I still live, I'm fine.

Listen for the old songs we loved so long ago
Think of me when they are played on your radio.
Look out for white feathers that find their way to you
They are a gift of hope, of strength, a gift from me to you.

Look forward to your future. Don't dwell upon the past
Cherish every moment is one thing I would ask.
Live your life, love, laugh a lot, for every time you do
I once again can love and laugh, for I still live through you.

When your time comes and you return, back to the other side
And mysteries of life reveal what earthly form does hide.
You'll see I kept my promise, through every tear you cried
For every step you walked in life, with you, I walked beside.

New Horizon

I have lived so many lives now
Worn so many faces.
Told the lies to keep it safe
And buried all the traces.

I get back up every time
But lies keep pulling down.
I've been kept here for far too long
So tired of being bound.

My soul, it has grown weary
Deception steals when it surrounds
BE CAREFUL what you promise
It could wear you to the ground.

Lately, I have found myself
Look up instead of down.
I look to greener pastures
Where the truth I seek is found.

I promise, God! I'm older now
Your lessons were profound.
I understand you cannot grow
Or build on fluid ground.

Possibilities present themselves
On each day's new horizon.
Before I, too, run out of time
I feel it's time to try one.

I picture now how life could be
Send me strength from up above
With God's good grace delivered,
Find a home that's filled with love.

There is nothing quite as beautiful
As a tender lover's kiss.
I must have paid the price by now
Dear Lord, just give me this.

Cv4love

I am not like all the others that you have met before
Who took just what they wanted, then bolted out the door.
The ones that said commitment was something they abhorred
As they took your love for granted, leaving you felt uncared for.
…Then without even one last glance, said, "See you…" No Encore.

As you've cried, you've realised, whilst broken, on the floor
All that glitters is not gold and you need something more.
You need someone who's caring, someone more mature
Who makes you feel you're beautiful, loved and so secure.

All I ask is one chance, if I may be so bold
To tell you that a heart like yours should never feel so cold.
I could never think that loving you would be a chore
Although I am not perfect, I would love you ever more.

I swear I would support you. I won't be cruel or mean
I swear I will do all I can to help you reach your dreams.
I promise I would treat you kind, be patient, loving too

I won't play games, mess with your head, I promise to see
You!

We could travel round the world, or we could go out dancing
Spend our nights at home alone with plenty of romancing.
I'll be foolish… for your laughter. I'll give you room to
Breathe
Support your crazy passions, whatever your heart needs.
I won't be cruel or judging or controlling… You are free.

I can be hard to live with. Yes, I do like 'freaky clean'
Mostly I am funny, calm, sometimes a drama queen.
I do believe that you and I would make quite a pair
I won't run if things get tough. I promise I'll be there.

I won't take you for granted. I'm not the kind to stray
Yes, I will hold your hand through all our rainy days.
I may seem quite fragile, but easily, I'm tough
The only thing to ask yourself: For you, am I enough?

I would seal our love with passion, with honour and respect
I swear to God! This promise… your love, I will protect.
The only thing I ask from you, is that you show your love
My heart is just as precious, but I'll give to you… in trust!

Autumn

Leaves are weary on the bough
Autumn whispers, now creep in.
Vibrancy once held in green
Fades gold, carnelian.

Brisk, chill winds grow stronger
Rustling seized from lonely trees.
Leaves snatched, captive in currents
Ride a random, blustery breeze.

Majestic colours swirl and rush
Sweep into vast, blue sky.
Embracing nature's charging force
Spin faster as they fly.

Momentum breaks, hues suspend
Adorning calmer skies.
Then gently drift, confetti-like
To meet, where others lie.

I amble over withered throngs
Crisply, the scrunching sounds.
Each step laments the ebbing cracks
Of broken, scattered crowds.

And further, in a distant glade
A startled squirrel stares.
Standing to attention
As to question 'who goes there'

Responding to unwelcome form
Forgoes its dig for treasure.
With tail still puffed, it scampers off
Chirring with pure displeasure.

The beauty and the brilliance
Showcasing this fine day.
Will soon turn dull and lifeless
As we head winter's way.

So let the autumn whispers creep
Its chatter holds no sway
For I behold its glory
And marvel at its play.

Winter

As winter blows its frosty kiss
On skies of silver-grey
We yearn for warmth now lost to us
Of golden summer days.

Diamond glints in icy drops
Drum on the windowpane
Outside, the wind snarls along
Defies all hope for change.

Reluctantly, we venture
Brave the cheerless ebb and flow
With might, we 'hunt and gather'
All dressed up like Eskimos.

With happy hearts, on our return
And laden with our wares
Again, we throw our 'PJS' on
To hibernate like bears.

Outside, on steely, glassy earth
A red robin dances there

Quickstepping through the flowers
Like a feathered Fred Astaire.

This hardy horde of crocuses
Stand proudly in the gloom
Their defiant blaze of colour
Foretells spring with every bloom.

The bleakness held in winter's grip
Will ease, then soon be gone
But, for now, I'll sit and listen
To the robin's fluting song.

Spring

Nature's springtime palette bursts
Through winter's hopeless ground.
And birthed, within each colour swell
Life force, renewed, is found.

Born in every flowers bloom
Held hopes again restore.
As season's promised gifts unveil
Reminds, that we endure.

A clement breeze sways the freeze
And coaxed by warming sun.
Landscapes, once grey and barren
Grow verdant, vibrant, strong.

Once hibernating, creatures
Wake from dormant sleep.
Globetrotting birds return, upsurge
Dawn's chorus song of tweets.

Farmers plough and till the land
For seeds that must be sown.
They slurry, fertilise the soil
So new crops may be grown.

Birthing season now delivers
God's creatures, great and small.
Sleepless farmers keep vigil
To aid and care for all.

The countryside now echoes
With the music of the land.
A melody of mooing calves
Operatic, baaing lambs.

As bluer skies resist night's touch
And warmth from sun grows strong.
Springtime's blessings validate
That life shall carry on.

Summer

The impatient summer sun
Streams through the windowpane.
Warmth felt in its keen greeting
Tempts us outside to play.

As whispers of its balmy breath
Sails skies of azure blue
The cloudless zenith's blinding
With its bright, resplendent hue.

Scantily, we dress
To join the flip-flopped throng.
Sun lotion smeared on chalk-white skin
Hair coiffed, sunglasses on.

Humidity assaults my skin
As I click-clack outside.
To see the graceful dancing
Of two flitting butterflies.

The heavy hum of lawnmowers
Drowns out the noisy street.
Excited kids chase ice-cream vans
Race with bare, dirty feet.

As sunshine-sparkles hide, then flash
Through leaves of swaying trees
Parched branches yield into the trance
Of summer's sultry breeze.

The smoky scents of barbecues
Blend with fragrant flowers.
Back gardens fill as friends meet up
To party, chat for hours.

I saunter to the seashore
Through the sticky, muggy day.
Lay down by the water's edge
To cool down, to sunbathe.

I am hypnotised with lullabies
Of rippling, swashing waves.
I drift, surrender to the mood
Of easy summer days.

Deathbed

Fast-forward time, See yourself
Upon your own deathbed.
Is peace found within your heart
Or wounded with regrets.

Does your smile display echoes?
Do you relish memory gifts?
If given time, would you rewind
Change the life you've lived?

Did your passions guide you
In pursuance of your dreams?
Did courage fail, leave you curtailed?
Compliant to mainstream?

Did you convey with patience
Tolerance and understanding
Or selfishly, in ignorance
Live bitter and demanding?

Did you honour your heart
Bestowed on those you love?
Did you leave them cherished
Or feeling scorned, unloved?

Was every moment savoured?
Were you wastefully resigned
Knowing, every one of us
Are captives – doomed in time?

If there's anything you harbour
Words your heart needs to say,
Express them now, while you can
Don't wait for Judgement Day.

To live true, be authentic
For life deemed a success
Know peace throughout your journey
Don't wait on your last breath.